Nutty

KNOCK-KNOCK JOKES for Kids

BOB PHILLIPS

HARVEST HOUSE PUBLISHERS

EUGENE, OREGON

Cover by Dugan Design Group, Bloomington, Minnesota

Cover illustration © Dugan Design Group

NUTTY KNOCK-KNOCK JOKES FOR KIDS
Copyright © 2009 by Bob Phillips
Published by Harvest House Publishers
Eugene, Oregon 97402
www.harvesthousepublishers.com

ISBN 978-0-7369-2615-7

Printed in the United States of America

09 10 11 12 13 14 15 16 17 / BP-SK / 10 9 8 7 6 5 4 3 2 1

CONTENTS

KNOCK, KNOCK!

Knock, knock.
Who's there?
Aaron.
Aaron who?
Aaron on the side of caution!

Knock, knock.
Who's there?
Abba.
Abba who?
Abba'out face! Now march!

Knock, knock.
Who's there?
Abbey.
Abbey who?
Abbey stung me on the nose!

5

Knock, knock.
Who's there?
Abbott.
Abbott who?
Abbott time you opened this door!

Knock, knock.
Who's there?
Abby.
Abby who?
Abby seeing you in all the old familiar places.

Knock, knock.
Who's there?
A bee.
A bee who?
A bee C D E F G H...!

Knock, knock.
Who's there?
Abel.
Abel who?
Abel to see you—ha, ha!

Knock, knock.
Who's there?
Abel.
Abel who?
Abel seaman!

Knock, knock.
Who's there?
Acid.
Acid who?
Acid here all day waiting for you.

Knock, knock.
Who's there?
Acis.
Acis who?
Acis spades!

Knock, knock.
Who's there?
Actor.
Actor who?
Actor up the contract.

Knock, knock.
Who's there?
Acute.
Acute who?
Acute little boy!

Knock, knock.
Who's there?
Ada.
Ada who?
Ada burger for lunch!

Knock, knock.
Who's there?
Adder.
Adder who?
Adder you get in here?

Knock, knock.
Who's there?
Adelia.
Adelia who?
Adelia the cards after you cut the deck!

Knock, knock.
Who's there?
Adolf.
Adolf who?
Adolf ball hit me in the mouth!

Knock, knock.
Who's there?
A Fred.
A Fred who?
Who's afred of the big bad wolf?

Knock, knock.
Who's there?
Agatha.
Agatha who?
Agatha headache. Do you have an aspirin?

Knock, knock.
Who's there?
Agent.
Agent who?
Agentle breeze!

Knock, knock.
Who's there?
Ahab.
Ahab who?
Ahab to go to the toilet now—quick! Open the door!

Knock, knock.
Who's there?
Ahmed.
Ahmed who?
Ahmed a big mistake coming here!

Knock, knock.
Who's there?
Ahmed.
Ahmed who?
Ahmedeus Mozart!

Knock, knock.
Who's there?
Aida.
Aida who?
Aida more than I drink!

WHO'S THERE?

Knock, knock.
Who's there?
B-4.
B-4 who?
B-4 I freeze to death, please open this door!

Knock, knock.
Who's there?
Bach.
Bach who?
Bach of candy!

Knock, knock.
Who's there?
Bacon.
Bacon who?
Bacon a cake for your birthday!

Knock, knock.
Who's there?
Badger.
Badger who?
Badger cookies!

Knock, knock.
Who's there?
Balanchine.
Balachine who?
Balachine act!

Knock, knock.
Who's there?
Balloon.
Balloon who?
Balloon velvet are pretty colors!

Knock, knock.
Who's there?
Banana.
Banana who?
Banana split so ice creamed!

Knock, knock.
Who's there?
Band.
Band who?
Band dancing all night!

Knock, knock.
Who's there?
Barbara.
Barbara who?
Barbara black sheep, have you any wool?

Knock, knock.
Who's there?
Barber.
Barber who?
Barber-d wire can scratch you real bad if you're
     not careful!

Knock, knock.
Who's there?
Barbie.
Barbie who?
Barbie Q!

Knock, knock.
Who's there?
Bar-B-Q.
Bar-B-Q who?
Bar-B-Q-t, but I think you're even cuter!

Knock, knock.
Who's there?
Bargain.
Bargain who?
Bargain up the wrong tree!

Knock, knock.
Who's there?
Bark.
Bark who?
Bark your car in the drive!

Knock, knock.
Who's there?
Baron.
Baron who?
Baron mind who you're talking to!

Knock, knock.
Who's there?
Barrister.
Barrister who?
Barristercratic!

Knock, knock.
Who's there?
Barry.
Barry who?
Barry the treasure where no one will find it!

Knock, knock.
Who's there?
Barry.
Barry who?
Barry your time capsule so someone will find it ten
    years from now!

Knock, knock.
Who's there?
Bart.
Bart who?
Bart up the wrong tree!

Knock, knock.
Who's there?
Bashful.
Bashful who?
I can't tell you. I'm so embarrassed!

Knock, knock.
Who's there?
Basis.
Basis who?
He was safe at home basis.

DO YOU HEAR THAT KNOCKING SOUND?

Knock, knock.
Who's there?
C-2.
C-2 who?
C-2 it that you don't forget my name next time!

Knock, knock.
Who's there?
Cab.
Cab who?
Cab is another name for a "taxi."

Knock, knock.
Who's there?
Caesar.
Caesar who?
Caesar quickly before she gets away!

Knock, knock.
Who's there?
Cain.
Cain who?
Cain you tell?

Knock, knock.
Who's there?
Caitlin.
Caitlin who?
Caitlin you my workout pants tonight. I'm wearing
    them!

Knock, knock.
Who's there?
Callas.
Callas who?
Callas should be removed by a foot doctor!

Knock, knock.
Who's there?
Callum.
Callum who?
Callum all cars! There's a robber in the area!

Knock, knock.
Who's there?
Cam.
Cam who?
Camelot is where King Arthur lived!

Knock, knock.
Who's there?
Camera.
Camera who?
Camera minute—I want to talk to you!

Knock, knock.
Who's there?
Cameron.
Cameron who?
Cameron film are needed to take pictures!

Knock, knock.
Who's there?
Candace.
Candace who?
Candace a pretty good polka!

Knock, knock.
Who's there?
Candice.
Candice who?
Candice get any better?

Knock, knock.
Who's there?
Candy.
Candy who?
Candy cow jump over the moon?

Knock, knock.
Who's there?
Cannelloni.
Cannelloni who?
Cannelloni some money till next week?

Knock, knock.
Who's there?
Canter.
Canter who?
Canter your sister come out to play?

Knock, knock.
Who's there?
Canto.
Canto who?
Canto your change and see if you have enough
    money!

Knock, knock.
Who's there?
Card.
Card who?
Card you see it's me?

Knock, knock.
Who's there?
Cargo.
Cargo who?
Cargo better if you fill it with gas first!

Knock, knock.
Who's there?
Cargo.
Cargo who?
Cargo "beep beep" and ran over my big toe!

Knock, knock.
Who's there?
Carlotta.
Carlotta who?
Carlotta trouble when it breaks down!

Knock, knock.
Who's there?
Carrie.
Carrie who?
Carrie the bags into the house, please!

Knock, knock.
Who's there?
Cash.
Cash who?
I didn't realize you were some kind of nut!

SOMEBODY'S AT THE DOOR!

Knock, knock.
Who's there?
D-1.
D-1 who?
D-1 who knocked!

Knock, knock.
Who's there?
Dad.
Dad who?
Dad fuel to the fire!

Knock, knock.
Who's there?
Daisy.
Daisy who?
Daisy that you are in, but I don't believe them!

Knock, knock.
Who's there?
Dali.
Dali who?
Dali've me alone!

Knock, knock.
Who's there?
Danny.
Danny who?
Dannybody home?

Knock, knock.
Who's there?
Danzig.
Danzig who?
Danzig queen who likes to waltz!

Knock, knock.
Who's there?
Darius.
Darius who?
Darius a lot I have to tell you!

Knock, knock.
Who's there?
Darwin.
Darwin who?
I'm Darwin you to open the door!

Knock, knock.
Who's there?
Daryl.
Daryl who?
Daryl never be another you!

Knock, knock.
Who's there?
Data.
Data who?
Data remember is my birthday.

Knock, knock.
Who's there?
Datsun.
Datsun who?
Datsun old knock-knock joke!

Knock, knock.
Who's there?
Daughter.
Daughter who?
Daughter be a law against people locking their door!

Knock, knock.
Who's there?
Dave.
Dave who?
Dave seen an image of your head and found
    nothing in it!

Knock, knock.
Who's there?
Dave.
Dave who?
Dave before yesterday I knocked on your door, and
    you didn't answer.

Knock, knock.
Who's there?
Dawn.
Dawn who?
Dawn do anything I wouldn't do!

Knock, knock.
Who's there?
Deanna.
Deanna who?
Deanna-mals are restless—open the cage!

Knock, knock.
Who's there?
Deanne.
Deanne who?
Deanne'swer my friend, is blowin' in the wind!

Knock, knock.
Who's there?
Debark.
Debark who?
Debark of your dog is too loud.

Knock, knock.
Who's there?
Debbie.
Debbie who?
Debbie or not to be...that is the question!

Knock, knock.
Who's there?
Debussy.
Debussy who?
Debussy's never on time!

Knock, knock.
Who's there?
Deceit.
Deceit who?
Deceit is taken—find your own seat!

Knock, knock.
Who's there?
Deduct.
Deduct who?
Donald Deduct!

Knock, knock.
Who's there?
Deena.
Deena who?
Deena hear me the first time?

Knock, knock.
Who's there
Delhi.
Delhi who?
Delhi me another knock-knock joke!

Knock, knock.
Who's there?
Delhi.
Delhi who?
Delhicatessen!

Knock, knock.
Who's there?
Delphine.
Delphine who?
Delphine fine, thanks!

Knock, knock.
Who's there?
Delta.
Delta who?
Delta great hand of cards!

Knock, knock.
Who's there?
Demi Moore.
Demi Moore who?
Demi Moore cake and ice cream please!

Knock, knock.
Who's there?
De Niro.
De Niro who?
De Niro the bear gets, the faster I run!

Knock, knock.
Who's there?
Denis.
Denis who?
Denis must be the right house?

Knock, knock.
Who's there?
Denver.
Denver who?
Denver the good old days!

COME IN!

Knock, knock.
Who's there
Eames.
Eames who?
I Eames to please!

Knock, knock.
Who's there?
Eamon.
Eamon who?
Eamon in a good mood today. Come in!

Knock, knock.
Who's there?
Ear.
Ear who?
Ear you are. I've been looking for you!

Knock, knock.
Who's there?
Earwig.
Earwig who?
Earwigo!

Knock, knock.
Who's there?
Ease.
Ease who?
Ease up to you to open the door!

Knock, knock.
Who's there?
Eaton.
Eaton who?
Eaton dessert is one of my favorite things.

Knock, knock.
Who's there?
Eaton.
Eaton who?
Eaton crow, and it doesn't taste good!

Knock, knock.
Who's there?
E.C.
E.C. who?
E.C. Street!

Knock, knock.
Who's there?
Eclipse.
Eclipse who?
Eclipse my hair because it is too long.

Knock, knock.
Who's there?
Ed.
Ed who?
Ed'vanced medicine for pain is what I need!

Knock, knock.
Who's there?
Eddie.
Eddie who?
Eddie body home?

Knock, knock.
Who's there?
Eddy.
Eddy who?
Eddy idea how to use this computer?

Knock, knock.
Who's there?
Eden.
Eden who?
Eden cherry pie à la mode is very tasty!

Knock, knock.
Who's there?
Edible.
Edible who?
Edible Rex is the name of a large chocolate dinosaur!

Knock, knock.
Who's there?
Edie.
Edie who?
Edie my hat because I was starving!

Knock, knock.
Who's there?
Edith.
Edith who?
Edith this pill. It'll make you feel better!

Knock, knock.
Who's there?
Edward.
Edward who?
Edward like to play now please!

Knock, knock.
Who's there?
Egbert.
Egbert who?
Egbert no bacon please!

Knock, knock.
Who's there?
Eight.
Eight who?
Eight me out of house and home!

Knock, knock.
Who's there?
Elaine.
Elaine who?
Elaine of the freeway!

Knock, knock.
Who's there?
Eli.
Eli who?
Eli, Eli O!

Knock, knock.
Who's there?
Eliza.
Eliza who?
Eliza wake at night thinking about this door.

Knock, knock.
Who's there?
Ella Man.
Ella Man who?
Ella Man-tary, my dear Watson!

Knock, knock.
Who's there?
Eudora.
Eudora who?
Eudora squeaks when it opens.

WHO'S OUTSIDE?

Knock, knock.
Who's there?
F-2.
F-2 who?
F-2 go to the bathroom!

Knock, knock.
Who's there?
Fajita.
Fajita who?
Fajita another thing I'm going to be sick!

Knock, knock.
Who's there?
Falafel.
Falafel who?
Falafel my bike and cut my knee!

Knock, knock.
Who's there?
Fang.
Fang who?
Fangs for letting me in!

Knock, knock.
Who's there?
Fang.
Fang who?
Fangs for the memory!

Knock, knock.
Who's there?
Fanny.
Fanny who?
Fanny body calls, I'm out!

Knock, knock.
Who's there?
Fanny.
Fanny who?
Fanny girl…you make me laugh!

Knock, knock.
Who's there?
Fanny.
Fanny who?
Fanny the way you keep saying "Who's there?"
    every time I knock!

Knock, knock.
Who's there?
Fanny.
Fanny who?
Fanny body home?

Knock, knock.
Who's there?
Fanta.
Fanta who?
Fanta Claus! Do you have your list ready?

Knock, knock.
Who's there?
Farley.
Farley who?
Farley the leader or you'll get lost!

Knock, knock.
Who's there?
Farmer.
Farmer who?
Farmer people here than there were last year!

Knock, knock.
Who's there?
Farmer.
Farmer who?
Farmer birthday I would like to have a new bike!

Knock, knock.
Who's there?
Farrah.
Farrah who?
Farrah 'nough, partner—don't draw your guns!

Knock, knock.
Who's there?
Fascist.
Fascist who?
Is this the Fascist you can go?

Knock, knock.
Who's there?
Fashion.
Fashion who?
Fashion your helmet in case you fall off of your bike.

Knock, knock.
Who's there?
Fasten.
Fasten who?
Fasten the draw!

Knock, knock.
Who's there?
Fatso.
Fatso who?
Fatso the matter with you—can't you hear me knocking?

Knock, knock.
Who's there?
Fax.
Fax who?
Fax you very much!

Knock, knock.
Who's there?
Fay Row.
Fay Row who?
Fay Row was buried in a pyramid.

Knock, knock.
Who's there?
Faye.
Faye who?
Faye all laughed when I spilled my milk!

Knock, knock.
Who's there?
Felipe.
Felipe who?
Felipe bathtub, I need a wash!

Knock, knock.
Who's there?
Felix.
Felix who?
Felixited about meeting you!

Knock, knock.
Who's there?
Felix.
Felix who?
Felix my ice cream, I'll lick his!

THE DOOR IS CLOSED!

Knock, knock.
Who's there?
Gabe.
Gabe who?
Gabe it my all!

Knock, knock.
Who's there?
Gable.
Gable who?
Gable to leap tall buildings in a single bound!

Knock, knock.
Who's there?
Gabor.
Gabor who?
I was Gabor'n to shop!

Knock, knock.
Who's there?
Gail.
Gail who?
Gail of laughter!

Knock, knock.
Who's there?
Gala.
Gala who?
Galafornia here I come!

Knock, knock.
Who's there?
Galahad.
Galahad who?
Galahad enough money to buy a car!

Knock, knock.
Who's there?
Galway.
Galway who?
Galway! I'm riding my skateboard though the crowd!

Knock, knock.
Who's there?
Galaway.
Galaway who?
Galaway! You're annoying me!

Knock, knock.
Who's there?
Gandhi.
Gandhi who?
Gandhi come out and play?

Knock, knock.
Who's there?
Gandhi.
Gandhi who?
Gandhi canes sure taste good!

Knock, knock.
Who's there?
Garden.
Garden who?
Garden the treasure so no one will steal it!

Knock, knock.
Who's there?
Gargoyle.
Gargoyle who?
Gargoyle with Listerine, and it will take away your
    bad breath.

Knock, knock.
Who's there?
Gary.
Gary who?
Gary on and do a good job!

Knock, knock.
Who's there?
Gaskills.
Gaskills who?
Gaskills if it's not turned off!

Knock, knock.
Who's there?
Gay.
Gay who?
Gay Topen, that's how the cows got out!

Knock, knock.
Who's there?
Gazza.
Gazza who?
Gazza kiss for me?

Knock, knock.
Who's there?
Genoa.
Genoa who?
Genoa good knock-knock joke you could tell me?

Knock, knock.
Who's there?
Geoff.
Geoff who?
Geoff feel like coming outside and playing?

Knock, knock.
Who's there?
George.
George who?
George-us day for going swimming!

Knock, knock.
Who's there?
Germaine.
Germaine who?
Germaine you don't recognize me?

Knock, knock.
Who's there?
Germany.
Germany who?
Germany people knocking on your door?

Knock, knock.
Who's there?
Gilda.
Gilda who?
Gilda umpire!

Knock, knock.
Who's there?
Gilda.
Gilda who?
Gilda fly that sat on the end of my nose!

Knock, knock.
Who's there?
Gina.
Gina who?
Gina you don't recognize me?

LET ME IN!

Knock, knock.
Who's there?
Hacienda.
Hacienda who?
Hacienda the story!

Knock, knock.
Who's there?
Haden.
Haden who?
Haden in the bushes so no one will catch me!

Knock, knock.
Who's there?
Haden.
Haden who?
Haden seek is a fun game to play!

Knock, knock.
Who's there?
Hagar.
Hagar who?
Hagar, you with the stars in your eyes…!

Knock, knock.
Who's there?
Hagen.
Hagen who?
Hagen Daz is sure good ice cream!

Knock, knock.
Who's there?
Haitit.
Haitit who?
Haitit when you tell all those knock-knock jokes!

Knock, knock.
Who's there?
Haji.
Haji who?
Haji'cken in every pot!

Knock, knock.
Who's there?
Hal.
Hal who?
Hal about you telling a knock-knock joke?

Knock, knock.
Who's there?
Hal.
Hal who?
Hallo to you too!

Knock, knock.
Who's there?
Hal.
Hal who?
Hallelujah chorus!

Knock, knock.
Who's there?
Halibut.
Halibut who?
Halibut letting me in on the secret?

Knock, knock.
Who's there?
Halibut.
Halibut who?
Halibut a kiss, sweetheart!

Knock, knock.
Who's there?
Hammond.
Hammond who?
Hammond eggs!

Knock, knock.
Who's there?
Hammond.
Hammond who?
Hammond cheese on toast, please!

Knock, knock.
Who's there?
Hand.
Hand who?
Hand over your money!

Knock, knock.
Who's there?
Hank.
Hank who?
You're welcome!

WHAT'S ALL THAT RACKET?

Knock, knock.
Who's there?
I-4.
I-4 who?
I-4 the ladies!

Knock, knock.
Who's there?
I-8.
I-8 who?
I-8 lunch already. Is dinner ready?

Knock, knock.
Who's there?
Ian.
Ian who?
Ian a lot of money!

Knock, knock.
Who's there?
Ice cream.
Ice cream who?
Ice cream if you don't let me in!

Knock, knock.
Who's there?
Ice cream.
Ice cream who?
Ice cream and scream and scream until I'm sick!

Knock, knock.
Who's there?
Ice cream.
Ice cream who?
Ice cream of Jeannie with the light brown hair!

Knock, knock.
Who's there?
Ice cream soda.
Ice cream soda who?
Ice cream soda whole world will know what a nut
    you are!

Knock, knock.
Who's there?
Ice water.
Ice water who?
Ice water bug in my glass.

Knock, knock.
Who's there?
Ichabod.
Ichabod who?
Ichabod night out—can I borrow an umbrella?

Knock, knock
Who's there?
Icing.
Icing who?
Icing in the school choir.

Knock, knock.
Who's there?
Icy.
Icy who?
Icy you in there! Open the door!

Knock, knock.
Who's there?
Ida.
Ida who?
Ida know why I love you like I do!

Knock, knock.
Who's there?
Ida.
Ida who?
Idaho, not Ida-who. Can't you say it correctly?

Knock, knock.
Who's there?
Ida.
Ida who?
Ida me! Ida me! Quick!

Knock, knock.
Who's there?
Ida.
Ida who?
Ida know. Sorry!

Knock, knock.
Who's there?
Ida.
Ida who?
Ida terrible time getting here!

Knock, knock.
Who's there?
Ida.
Ida who?
Ida bought a better knocker if I were you!

Knock, knock.
Who's there?
Idaho.
Idaho who?
Idaho'd the whole garden but I was tired!

Knock, knock.
Who's there?
I don't know!
I don't know who?
I told you I don't know. Why don't you believe me?

Knock, knock.
Who's there?
Iglesias.
Iglesias who?
Iglesias idea I ever had!

Knock, knock.
Who's there?
Igloo.
Igloo who?
Igloo knew Suzie like I know Suzie…!

Knock, knock.
Who's there?
Iguana.
Iguana who?
Iguana hold your hand!

Knock, knock.
Who's there?
Ike.
Ike who?
Ike-ant stop laughing at these knock-knock jokes!

Knock, knock.
Who's there?
Ike.
Ike who?
Ike could have danced all night!

Knock, knock.
Who's there?
Legal.
Legal who?
Legals stay in the nest until they feel better!

Knock, knock.
Who's there?
Ima.
Ima who?
Ima girl who can't say no to ice cream!

Knock, knock.
Who's there?
Imogen.
Imogen who?
Imogen life without chocolate!

I'M NOT HOME!

Knock, knock.
Who's there?
Jack.
Jack who?
Jack through the peephole and find out!

Knock, knock.
Who's there?
Jack.
Jack who?
I won the jackpot!

Knock, knock.
Who's there?
Jack.
Jack who?
Jack needed? I see that one of your tires is flat!

Knock, knock.
Who's there?
Jackie.
Jackie who?
Jackie is what you wear when it is cold outside!

Knock, knock.
Who's there?
Jackson.
Jackson who?
Jackson the telephone—you'd better answer it!

Knock, knock.
Who's there?
Jackson.
Jackson who?
Jackson is also the son of his wife.

Knock, knock.
Who's there?
Jacqueline.
Jacqueline who?
Jacqueline and Hyde! Pretty scary, huh?

Knock, knock.
Who's there?
Jacques.
Jacques who?
Jacques of all trades!

Knock, knock.
Who's there?
Jade.
Jade who?
Jade a whole pizza today!

Knock, knock.
Who's there?
Jagger.
Jagger who!
Jagger'd edge is on the knife. Watch out!

Knock, knock.
Who's there?
Jaguar.
Jaguar who?
Jaguar nimble, Jaguar quick!

Knock, knock.
Who's there?
Jaimie.
Jaimie who?
Jaimie a game of chess!

Knock, knock.
Who's there?
Jakal.
Jakal who?
Jakal get in if he has a key.

Knock, knock.
Who's there?
Jam.
Jam who?
Jam mind? I'm trying to get out!

Knock, knock.
Who's there?
Jamaica.
Jamaica who?
Jamaica mistake?

Knock, knock.
Who's there?
Jamaica.
Jamaica who?
Jamaica me listen to too many knock-knock jokes.

Knock, knock.
Who's there?
James.
James who?
James people play can be pretty crazy!

Knock, knock.
Who's there?
Jamie.
Jamie who?
Jamie'n…you don't recognize my voice?

Knock, knock.
Who's there?
Jan.
Jan who?
Jan of Green Gables!

Knock, knock.
Who's there?
Janet.
Janet who?
Janet has too many holes in it. The fish will escape!

Knock, knock.
Who's there?
Janet.
Janet who?
Janet'or in a drum!

Knock, knock.
Who's there?
Japan.
Japan who?
Japan is too hot! Ouch!

Knock, knock.
Who's there?
Jasmine.
Jasmine who?
Jasmine like to play in quartets!

Knock, knock.
Who's there?
Jason.
Jason who?
Jason a rainbow won't get you to a pot of gold!

Knock, knock.
Who's there?
Java.
Java who?
Java dog in your house!

Knock, knock.
Who's there?
Jay.
Jay who?
Jay've been chasing me for a while.

Knock, knock.
Who's there?
Jean.
Jean who?
I'm a Jeanius...you just don't recognize it!

Knock, knock.
Who's there?
Jeff.
Jeff who?
Jeff in one ear. You'll have to shout!

NO MORE VISITORS!

Knock, knock.
Who's there?
K-2.
K-2 who?
K-2 come in?

Knock, knock.
Who's there?
Kai.
Kai who?
My kai flies in the sky on windy days!

Knock, knock.
Who's there?
Kanga.
Kanga who?
No, Kangaroo!

Knock, knock.
Who's there?
Kareem.
Kareem who?
His basketball team got kareemed last night and
    lost the game.

Knock, knock.
Who's there?
Kareem.
Kareem who?
Kareem of the crop!

Knock, knock.
Who's there?
Karen.
Karen who?
Karen heavy bags is hard work!

Knock, knock.
Who's there?
Karsen.
Karsen who?
Karsen the parking lot. Do you have enough money
    to get it out?

Knock, knock.
Who's there?
Katherine.
Katherine who?
Katherine the Queen of England!

Knock, knock.
Who's there?
Kathy.
Kathy who?
Kathy you again!

Knock, knock.
Who's there?
Katie.
Katie who?
Katie is a tea party for people with names that start
    with K.

Knock, knock.
Who's there?
Katie.
Katie who?
Katie Lang!

Knock, knock.
Who's there?
Kay.
Kay who?
Kay, L, M, N, O, P, Q, R, S, T, U, V, W, X, Y, Z!

Knock, knock.
Who's there?
Keanu.
Keanu who?
Keanu let me in? It's cold out here!

Knock, knock.
Who's there?
Keanu.
Keanu who?
Keanu hear me knocking?

Knock, knock.
Who's there?
Keith.
Keith who?
Keith your hands off of me!

Knock, knock.
Who's there?
Kelda.
Kelda who?
Kelda a rattlesnake before it bit me.

Knock, knock.
Who's there?
Ken.
Ken who?
Ken you open the door and let me in?

Knock, knock.
Who's there?
Ken.
Ken who?
Ken I come in? I've been waiting here all day!

GO AWAY!

Knock, knock.
Who's there?
L.A.
L.A. who?
L.A. down for a snooze and slept all afternoon!

Knock, knock.
Who's there?
Lacey.
Lacey who?
He's Lacey as the day is long!

Knock, knock.
Who's there?
Lady.
Lady who?
Lady law down!

Knock, knock.
Who's there?
Lana.
Lana who?
Lana the free and the home of the brave!

Knock, knock.
Who's there?
Lara.
Lara who?
Lara lara laughs with these knock-knock jokes!

Knock, knock.
Who's there?
Lazy.
Lazy who?
Lazy key on the table where I can find it.

Knock, knock.
Who's there?
Leaf.
Leaf who?
Leaf me alone!

Knock, knock.
Who's there?
Leah.
Leah who?
Leah-n an egg for my breakfast!

Knock, knock.
Who's there?
Lecture.
Lecture who?
Lecture smile be your first hello!

Knock, knock.
Who's there?
Lee.
Lee who?
Lee me alone! I've got a headache!

Knock, knock.
Who's there?
Leena.
Leena who?
Leena too far over the wall and you'll fall on your head!

Knock, knock.
Who's there?
Lenny.
Lenny who?
Lenny in. I'm hungry!

Knock, knock.
Who's there?
Leon.
Leon who?
Leon'ly one for me!

KNOCK IT OFF!

Knock, knock.
Who's there?
Mabel.
Mabel who?
Mabel on my door doesn't ring either!

Knock, knock.
Who's there?
Mabel.
Mabel who?
Mabel syrup is great on hot cakes!

Knock, knock.
Who's there?
Madge.
Madge who?
Madge you ask...didn't I?

Knock, knock.
Who's there?
Madonna.
Madonna who?
Madonna's being mean. Tell her off!

Knock, knock.
Who's there?
Madrid.
Madrid who?
Madrid you wash my jeans?

Knock, knock.
Who's there?
Mae.
Mae who?
Mae be I'll tell you or Mae be I won't!

Knock, knock.
Who's there?
Maggot.
Maggot who?
Maggot me these new jeans today!

Knock, knock.
Who's there?
Maia.
Maia who?
Maia hand is sore from knocking!

Knock, knock.
Who's there?
Maia.
Maia who?
Maianimals are like children to me!

Knock, knock.
Who's there?
Major.
Major who?
Major B. Hindsor when you got spanked!

Knock, knock.
Who's there?
Major.
Major who?
Major headache from all these knock-knock jokes!

JUST A SECOND!

Knock, knock.
Who's there?
N-8.
N-8 who?
I have N-8 tendencies to tell knock-knock jokes!

Knock, knock.
Who's there?
Nach.
Nach who?
Nach me for a loop!

Knock, knock.
Who's there?
Nadia.
Nadia who?
Nadia head if you like this joke!

Knock, knock.
Who's there?
Nadya.
Nadya who?
Nadya head if you understand what I'm saying!

Knock, knock.
Who's there?
Nan.
Nan who?
Nanswer me or I'll go away!

Knock, knock.
Who's there?
Nana.
Nana who?
Nana, nana, nana! Guess who yourself!

Knock, knock.
Who's there?
Nana.
Nana who?
Nana your business!

Knock, knock.
Who's there?
Nanny.
Nanny who?
Nanny one at home?

Knock, knock.
Who's there?
Nanny.
Nanny who?
Nanny people are waiting to come in!

Knock, knock.
Who's there?
Nantucket.
Nantucket who?
Nantucket, but she'll have to give it back!

I'M NOT OPENING THE DOOR!

Knock, knock.
Who's there?
Obi Wan.
Obi Wan who?
Obi Wan of the good guys! Let me in!

Knock, knock.
Who's there?
Odessa.
Odessa who?
Odessa really funny joke!

Knock, knock.
Who's there?
Odessa.
Odessa who?
Odessa hot one, isn't it?

Knock, knock.
Who's there?
Oil change.
Oil change who?
Oil change my shoes and be back in a minute!

Knock, knock.
Who's there?
Oily.
Oily who?
The oily bird catches the worm!

ANYBODY HOME?

Knock, knock.
Who's there?
P.
P who?
P nuts are an elephant's favorite treat!

Knock, knock.
Who's there?
Pablo.
Pablo who?
Pablo your horn!

Knock, knock.
Who's there?
Paine.
Paine who?
Paine in the neck!

Knock, knock.
Who's there?
Pam.
Pam who?
Pam-per yourself!

Knock, knock.
Who's there?
Pammy.
Pammy who?
Pammy the key so I can get in!

Knock, knock.
Who's there?
Panel.
Panel who?
Panel hold soup for lunch.

Knock, knock.
Who's there?
Panon.
Panon who?
Panon the stove is burning...you better put it out!

Knock, knock.
Who's there?
Panther.
Panther who?
Panther what you wear on your legs!

STOP BEATING THE DOOR DOWN!

Knock, knock.
Who's there?
Quack.
Quack who?
Quack an egg and fry it in the skillet.

Knock, knock.
Who's there?
Quacker.
Quacker who?
Quacker another bad joke and I'm leaving!

Knock, knock.
Who's there?
Quick.
Quick who?
Quick telling me these jokes.

Knock, knock.
Who's there?
Quiet.
Quiet who?
Quiet a long ride to the ocean.

Knock, knock.
Who's there ?
Quiet Tina.
Quiet Tina who?
Quiet Tina courtroom—monkey wants to speak!

TAP, TAP, TAP!

Knock, knock.
Who's there?
Ralph.
Ralph who?
Ralph! Ralph! Ralph! I'm your puppy-dog!

Knock, knock.
Who's there?
Randy.
Randy who?
Randy four minute mile!

Knock, knock.
Who's there?
Rattlesnake.
Rattlesnake who?
Rattlesnake will bite you if you're not careful!

Knock, knock.
Who's there?
Ray.
Ray who?
Ray drops keep falling on my head!

USE THE DOORBELL!

Knock, knock.
Who's there?
Sabina.
Sabina who?
Sabina a long time since I've seen you!

Knock, knock.
Who's there?
Sacha.
Sacha who?
Sacha lot of questions!

Knock, knock.
Who's there?
Sacha.
Sacha who?
Sacha fuss, just because I knocked on your door!

Knock, knock.
Who's there?
Sadie.
Sadie who?
Sadie ten times table twice!

Knock, knock.
Who's there?
Sadie.
Sadie who?
Sadie Pledge of Allegiance!

Knock, knock.
Who's there?
Safari.
Safari who?
Safari so good!

Knock, knock.
Who's there?
Saffron.
Saffron who?
Saffron a chair and it collapsed!

Leave Me Alone!

Knock, knock.
Who's there?
Tad.
Tad who?
Tad's all, folks!

Knock, knock.
Who's there?
Tailor.
Tailor who?
Tailor to open the door right now!

Knock, knock.
Who's there?
Taipei.
Taipei who?
Taipei sixty words a minute is pretty fast!

Knock, knock.
Who's there?
Talbot.
Talbot who?
Talbot going roller skating with me?

Knock, knock.
Who's there?
Tamara.
Tamara who?
Tamara is Tuesday, today is Monday!

Knock, knock.
Who's there?
Tamara.
Tamara who?
Tamara I'm going to get an ax and break down
    your door!

YOU'RE GIVING ME A HEADACHE!

Knock, knock.
Who's there?
U-2.
U-2 who?
U-2 can buy a brand-new car for only $199 a month!

Knock, knock.
Who's there?
U-4.
U-4 who?
U-4 me and me for you!

Knock, knock.
Who's there?
U-8.
U-8 who?
U-8 my lunch!

Knock, knock.
Who's there?
U-boat.
U-boat who?
U-boat can play with me today!

Knock, knock.
Who's there?
UB40.
UB40 who?
UB40 today—happy birthday!

Knock, knock.
Who's there?
UCI.
UCI who?
UCI had to ring because you didn't answer when I
    knocked!

Knock, knock.
Who's there?
Udder.
Udder who?
Udder madness to keep reading all these jokes!

STOP COMING TO MY DOOR!

Knock, knock.
Who's there?
Valencia.
Valencia who?
Valencia dollar, will you pay it back?

Knock, knock.
Who's there?
Value.
Value who?
Value be my Valentine?

Knock, knock.
Who's there?
Vampire.
Vampire who?
Vampire State Building is very tall!

Knock, knock.
Who's there?
Vanda.
Vanda who?
Vanda you vant me to come around?

Knock, knock.
Who's there?
Vanessa.
Vanessa who?
Vanessa bus going to come?

Knock, knock.
Who's there?
Vanessa.
Vanessa who?
Vanessa time I'll ring the bell!

Knock, knock.
Who's there?
Vanessa.
Vanessa who?
Vanessa going to stop telling these jokes?

NO MORE KNOCK-KNOCKS, PLEASE!

Knock, knock.
Who's there?
Waddle.
Waddle who?
Waddle you give me if I go away?

Knock, knock.
Who's there?
Waddle.
Waddle who?
Waddle you do if I keep on telling these knock-
    knock jokes?

Knock, knock.
Who's there?
Wade.
Wade who?
Wade up, little Susie!

Knock, knock.
Who's there?
Wade.
Wade who?
Wade in the water and your feet will get wet!

Knock, knock.
Who's there?
Wade.
Wade who?
Wade till next time!

Knock, knock.
Who's there?
Wafer.
Wafer who?
Wafer too long and I'll play with someone else!

KNOCK ON SOMEBODY ELSE'S DOOR!

Knock, knock.
Who's there?
X.
X who?
X-tremely pleased to meet you!

Knock, knock.
Who's there?
X.
X who?
X-tra, X-tra, read all about it!

Knock, knock.
Who's there?
X.
X who?
X for asking!

Knock, knock.
Who's there?
Xavier.
Xavier who?
Xavier breath. I'm not leaving!

Knock, knock.
Who's there?
Xavier.
Xavier who?
Xavier your money for a rainy day!

Knock, knock.
Who's there?
Xena.
Xena who?
Xena minute I'll go away!

Knock, knock.
Who's there?
Xenia.
Xenia who?
Xenia stealing my candy!

YOU HAVE THE WRONG ADDRESS!

Knock, knock.
Who's there?
Ya.
Ya who?
I didn't know you were a cowboy!

Knock, knock.
Who's there?
Yacht.
Yacht who?
Yacht a know me by now!

Knock, knock.
Who's there?
Yachts.
Yachts who?
Yachts up, doc?

Knock, knock.
Who's there?
Yoga.
Yoga who?
Yoga what it takes!

ANSWER THE DOOR!

Knock, knock.
Who's there?
Zaire.
Zaire who?
Zaire is polluted!

Knock, knock.
Who's there?
Zany.
Zany who?
Zany body home?

Knock, knock.
Who's there?
Zeke.
Zeke who?
Zeke and you shall find!

Knock, knock.
Who's there?
Zena.
Zena who?
Zena you stealing my books!

Knock, knock.
Who's there?
Zenia.
Zenia who?
Zenia you on TV in that commercial!

Knock, knock.
Who's there?
Zephyr.
Zephyr who?
Zephyr de doctor, I got a code id by doze!

Other Books by Bob Phillips

*All-Time Awesome Collection
of Good Clean Jokes for Kids*

*The Awesome Book
of Bible Trivia*

*The Awesome Book
of Heavenly Humor*

*Awesome Good Clean
Jokes for Kids*

*Awesome Knock-Knock
Jokes for Kids*

*The Best of the Good
Clean Jokes*

Bible Trivia for Every Day

Dude, Got Another Joke?

*Extremely Good Clean
Jokes for Kids*

*Fabulous and Funny
Clean Jokes for Kids*

*Flat-Out Awesome Knock-
Knock Jokes for Kids*

*Good Clean Jokes to Drive
Your Parents Crazy*

*Good Clean Knock-Knock
Jokes for Kids*

How Can I Be Sure?

*How to Deal with
Annoying People*

*A Joke a Day Keeps the
Doctor Away*

Jolly Jokes for Older Folks

*Laughter from
the Pearly Gates*

Over the Hill & On a Roll

*Over the Next Hill
& Still Rolling*

*Over the Top Clean
Jokes for Kids*

*Overcoming Anxiety
and Depression*

*Super Incredible Knock-Knock
Jokes for Kids*

*The World's Greatest
Collection of Clean Jokes*

*The World's Greatest
Knock-Knock Jokes for Kids*

For more information, send a self-addressed
stamped envelope to:

Family Services
P.O. Box 9363
Fresno, California 93702